T0068148

One Shoe In Africa

WINSTON'S STORY

Winston Matafwali

WESTBOW
PRESS®
A DIVISION OF THOMAS NELSON
& ZONDERVAN

WestBow Press books may be ordered through booksellers or by contacting:

WestBow Press
A Division of Thomas Nelson & Zondervan
1663 Liberty Drive
Bloomington, IN 47403
www.westbowpress.com
844-714-3454

ISBN: 978-1-6642-5506-7 (sc)
ISBN: 978-1-6642-5508-1 (hc)
ISBN: 978-1-6642-5507-4 (e)

Library of Congress Control Number: 2022901844

Print information available on the last page.

WestBow Press rev. date: 02/22/2022

I am proud to dedicate this book One Shoe in Africa to Mrs. Gloria Jones, this great, white woman I used to call "mother" for the hope, joy, and abundance of love she brought to my life.

I am so saddened she didn't live to see this book.

Contents

Contents

Introduction

One Shoe in Africa is the story of how I struggled as a young person to come to terms with my disability. As an African child from a very poor family, I was struck by polio at the age of two years and was left paralyzed from the hips down. I could not walk at all.

For a long time, I was angry about this, and I deeply resented what seemed to me an unfair stroke of fate. What a difference it made when I finally accepted myself as a physically challenged person.

This book is also about my spiritual journey as a young and immature child of God, and how one missing shoe connected me to a life-long friend, Gloria Jones, who helped me to see the hand of God upon my life.

My story is also about how God uses good, bad,

and even the ugly situations in our life, to show His strength through His plans for us (which we rarely, if ever, understand until we look back many years later.)

Winston Matafwali

Preface

Zambia, Africa

2018

As the plane came to a stop on the tarmac, my heart began racing.

I realized the next few moments would take me on a journey I had dreamed of since I was 10 years old.

Africa…I had made it.

Finally!

My husband looked at me and smiled.

"You've waited for this for a long time, haven't you?"

Smiling from ear-to-ear I replied, "God is so good."

As we departed the plane, I could hardly contain myself. The person my husband and I had grown to love brought us to this continent. We had come to see our "African son" as he called himself.

I had always had an interest and curiosity about Africa and now, even more importantly, my husband and I would be spending the next few weeks with our dear Winston and his family.

My mind immediately thought of Gloria Jones, who was still in Florida. If our paths had not crossed in this life, this time would never have arrived. Because of her love and support of Winston, Mrs. Jones had prepared a way for this visit to Zambia.

And suddenly, there he was...all smiles. Sitting tall in his wheelchair and holding out his arms to welcome us. With tears streaming down my face, all I could say was "Thank You God, thank you."

"Thank you, Gloria," I whispered.

* * *

Having retired from teaching at Illinois State University, my also-retired husband and I moved to the sunny south, to Sebastian, located on the east coast of central Florida.

We became involved in The United Church of Sebastian where we made many new friends. I began a ladies' Bible study and made the acquaintance of one very talented lady who had recently moved to Sebastian from Africa.

My long interest in Africa was immediately renewed and I asked Mrs. Gloria Jones question after question. I hung on every word and thoroughly enjoyed her fantastic stories about living in Africa.

Gloria was so gracious about sharing details of her life with me and our Florida congregation. She explained the way people of means shared with the poor people in Zambia. They simply placed anything they wanted to share outside the walls lining their compounds.

The people in need would then walk up and down the compound walls to gather what they needed. It was a common practice during that time.

Julie (Hale) Maschhoff

Larry Maschhoff, Winston Jr., Julie Maschhoff, Jones at airport in Zambia.

The Story of One Shoe

I heard my house servant approach and say, "Mrs. Jones, there is a lady at the gate who would like to speak to you. She says thank you for the box of shoes, but she has a question for you."

Laying aside my book, I went to the back gate of our compound. The African woman looked at me shyly.

"Thank you, madam for all the things you leave here for us. We are poor and we use everything you leave. But, in the box of shoes you left here last week, one shoe is missing. Do you think it could be in your house somewhere? I am so sorry to ask you but..."

"Do not worry, I will be glad to look in the house. If your children need shoes, we will find the other shoe. Can you return tomorrow?"

"Oh, yes, madam, yes. We will come tomorrow."

That interaction with the African mother who was seeking shoes for her children seemed of little importance, at the time.

Due to my husband's work, we have lived all over the world, and I always tried to share things with those in need. I had left many boxes outside of my gates all over the world, but this box, with one shoe missing, changed my life in a way that I couldn't have imagined.

The next day, the lady returned for the shoe, (which I could not find). She was pushing a wheelbarrow. Inside the wheelbarrow sat a little boy with the biggest, brightest eyes I had ever seen. The minute I saw him, I felt a connection with him. I fell in love with this little boy.

"Oh my, what a darling child," I said to his mother. "He is adorable."

"Thank you, madam. His name is Winston."

I wondered why he sat so still. Most children run and jump about.

"Madam, he has polio and cannot walk."

My eyes filled with tears.

At that moment, Winston stole my heart.

Gloria Jones

*   *   *

If Only I Knew

The transition. Moving from the "Why me?" question that used to bother me so much to "Why not me?" was life changing.

I come from a family of nine children, the second-born of the Protasho and Juliet Matafwali family.

I was born July 31, 1968. My dad was so excited to have me as his first son, so much so that he gave me all his favorite names – Winston, Musanga, Matafwali, Churchill.

But all that changed when I became disabled because of polio. He renamed me "Washama," which in our native language means "the cursed one."

I understand now. He must have been so hurt and disappointed by what had happened to me. Even as a little boy, I felt that my father did not like me, and never thought anything good would ever become of me.

It was in this very city, Kitwe, when I was about two years old, that I got so sick, to a point of death. I was admitted in Kitwe Central Hospital.

I was struck by poliomyelitis, which left me with both legs paralyzed. Nobody really knows how it all started. All I am told is that after I had a bit of diarrhea during the day, we went to bed and the next morning I could not stand up nor walk anymore. Later, when I was taken to the hospital, it was confirmed that I had polio.

Poliomyelitis, as I have learned now, is a disease caused by the polio virus. This disease was common in children before the practice of immunization.

A person can, however, get the disease if one eats food or drinks water contaminated with the polio virus. When one swallows the virus and it gets into the intestine, it will cause damage to the intestinal wall cell's lining, causing diarrhea.

Then after reproducing itself, it will migrate from the intestines into the motor neuron cells in the spinal cord, causing damage to the nervous system that supplies the muscles. Because of this destruction, it may affect a limb or the respiratory muscles, sometimes even resulting in death.

Polio was responsible for many deaths and disabling of many people in the early 20th century.

My people tried conventional and traditional medicines, hoping that would help me, and put me on my feet again, but to no avail.

Mother would tell me that during this time I became very depressed. Society was not as sympathetic to a family with someone disabled as it is now.

In most cases, disability was considered punishment from God, so I was looked at as a curse, not only on myself, but on my parents. They were looked at as cursed people too.

What is even worse, I was looked at as someone without a future. The attitude that people displayed toward my mother was this: my family had brought a burden into the community - a curse, not a blessing.

Women, because they are the ones with the womb and they carry the baby for some months, get much of the blame for disabled children. A poor mother is no exception. What was happening in my family was looked at as punishment from God for something my mother might have done.

Sadly, my father was not supportive. He too blamed my mother for my disability. To make matters worse, he even deserted her at some point, leaving my mother alone to look after me and everyone else in the family. All because of me. Thank God he did come back after some time.

I remember my mother telling me also that it was not easy for her to carry me or take me anywhere with her. Whenever she did that, and my tiny legs were exposed, other women in the marketplace or in the streets would always whisper and laugh behind her back.

As a result, she usually did not take me out with her anywhere. I would be left home, most of the time alone. I grew up lonely and depressed because my brothers and sisters would go out to play but I remained at home.

What was even more disheartening is that other parents were not allowing their children to come near me. Worse still, those parents would not allow their children to play with me because I was "cursed."

I vividly remember one day (I must have been about

four or five years old) a young boy of my age came home to play with me. I was so excited that at last I had a friend.

But my joy was cut short when his father saw him and realized that he was playing with me. He even warned the boy never to come anywhere near me again.

I was there watching, confused about what was happening as I listened to what was said. As if that was not enough, I noticed some difference in the way I was treated by the rest of my family members.

It is hurtful to grow up in a community where people do not like you. It's even more difficult to be in a family and a home where you are not loved enough.

My father did not like me at all. My mother was trying her best, and I would feel her love, but I also wanted to see Dad make an effort to accept me too. Especially because I was a boy, I missed him and longed for him. Even as a little boy, I could feel the lack and realized it was because I was disabled.

I slowly began to convince myself that perhaps I did not measure up to what was required of a normal human being and judged myself as being different and deficient.

I thought I lacked what it takes to deserve a better life, and eventually developed self-pity. For example, when taking a bath, I would often cry because when I would undress and have a good look at how deformed my body was. I would feel sorry for myself and cry uncontrollably.

When I looked at myself as a disabled person, I felt that I was worthless and not good enough to live. I became very bitter because I could not accept myself or forgive others for causing me pain. I was bitter at God for allowing this disability to happen to me.

These feelings of unworthiness and of not being good enough, as I compared myself to others who were better and strong, were the most devastating moments in my early childhood.

It is important to state that I was introduced to Christianity and God at a tender age. But it did not make much sense because I could not understand why a loving God, the Almighty, would allow me, as young as I was, to go through all the pain I was experiencing.

My cry to God was always "Why me, oh God?" Bitterness, self-pity, and loneliness took a deep root in me. I felt so empty, as if I had very little to live for. Was I really cursed as my other name, "Washama" suggested? If not, why were people looking down on me?

Little did I know that in this same "package" called disability, God would one day use me. If only I had known, then!

I feel I should provide some information about my country and several details about my family, so that you, the reader will better understand my story.

Zambia is administratively divided into 10 provinces: Luapula, Northern, Muchinga, Eastern, Central, Lusaka, Southern, Western, North- Western and the Copperbelt.

My father comes from Luapula Province of Zambia in Chilubi Islands of Lake Bangweulu, in Samfya district. His father (my grandfather) known as Musanga Matafwali, was a well-known trader and businessman on the island of Chilubi and his mother, my grandmother, was known as Chisala Matafwali. She was a bit reserved but a very loving person.

My father's people then lived solely on fishing and working on the land growing crops like cassava, yam and groundnuts (peanuts).

Zambia then was undeveloped, except a few places where the early white pioneers settled. Because of the rich deposits of copper and cobalt on the Copperbelt province, this area was better off than most places in the country.

The copper mines, as well as the other industries created by the Europeans in and around Copperbelt province, attracted a lot of people coming from every corner of Zambia who came to look for employment opportunities.

Education during my father's time was mostly through Christian mission schools. The African people were not compelled to attend school in their early years. However, it was compulsory for the European children to attend school.

My father was fortunate enough to have managed to attend school up to standard four (4). He was able to speak and write in English very well.

When he could not continue school due to financial support, my father decided to come to the Copperbelt to look for employment. His first job was that of a domestic helper. He was trained to keep or maintain the house clean, wash and cook for the white people.

It was during this time when dad had left his home village, Chilubi Islands, and came to live in Mufulira town in the Copperbelt. He met my mother and got married. After they had their first daughter, my elder sister Clara, my parents decided to move to the city of Kitwe where I was born in 1968.

Apart from working as a domestic worker for some time, especially in the colonial days before Zambia got its independence from the British in 1964, my father also worked for many years as a salesman for a big company known as Radio Limited.

It was the only company supplying radios and televisions in the Copperbelt those days. When he left Radio Limited, he joined Central Africa Engineering where he served as stores man in Chingola town in the Copperbelt until he retired in 1984.

The House We Lived In

The house we lived in was very tiny for a family of nine children. In most cases we all occupied a two-roomed house. These houses, although rented, had no kitchen. As I can remember, cooking was done outside on the veranda, on a brazier with charcoal. The two rooms were only a bedroom and a living room.

Our parents took the bedroom, and the children had the living room. We slept in the living room on the floor without even a mattress, making use of every available space at night.

Winston's wife, Tizi, works with community members to gather ground nuts (peanuts) at Winston's five-acre farm outside of Kitwe.

Mothers and Children

God sometimes gives us a second or
even a third and fourth chance.

Hardly a year after I was discovered to have polio, I fell seriously ill again. I would have been about three years old. It all started as malaria, but later I had difficulty breathing on my own.

When I was taken to the hospital, I was immediately put on an artificial respiration machine. Kitwe Central Hospital in Zambia, where I was admitted, was at that time overcrowded with many children who were sick. Some of them had to sleep on the floor. Because of my serious condition, I was lucky enough to be given a bed to sleep on, but still I had to share that bed with someone else.

My grandmother was by my bedside that night, and she had asked my mother to take a little rest at the mother's shelter at the hospital. This was a place where mothers who had their children admitted to the hospital, and had come from distant places, would sleep and prepare their meals. However, they were required to find their own food and had to sleep on the floor because there were no beds for them.

The boy that I was sharing the bed with was much better than I was, and he was breathing normally. It seemed that he was going to be discharged soon.

Sadly, early that morning that very boy died. When my mother heard people crying and wailing from that same ward, she nearly collapsed, and her heart was beating fast, thinking that it was I who just died.

To her surprise, she discovered it was not me but the other boy. The mother of the boy who died was so confused and devastated, she even picked a quarrel with my mum, angry in her despair. She was puzzled because it was I who was seriously ill. She must have thought: *How then was I still alive when she had lost her son?*

I do sympathize with her because if it had not been

for the Lord, I would have been dead. Yet, I still had the artificial breathing machine on me, even as the argument was going on.

God sometimes gives us a second or even a third and fourth chance. It is the intention of God that we should trust Him and believe in Him always and live with the faith that He is in control.

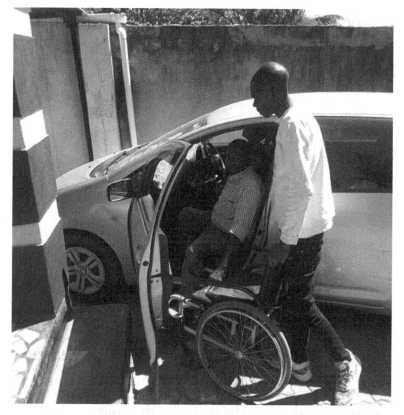

Winston and Tizi in the car with assistance from their son Jones.

I Would Not Have Gone To School

Had it not been for my uncle, who came in and helped me to get started, I really do not know what would have happened to me.

My life was so miserable and lonely. I was kept isolated at home as if people were only waiting for me to die. My parents were not doing anything to ease my disability or my life. I had no wheelchair but used to crawl to get about. My legs were folding up because I lacked those exercises you do with the help of a therapist.

The time for starting school was passing by, and my father, as usual, did not show any interest in taking me to school. He did not see any need for that. My father thought it would be a waste of time and resources, because he and many others thought that I was not going to live long.

The rest of my siblings were taken to school, but I was not. It took my uncle coming in and taking me from my parents by force.

My uncle came and collected me from my parent's home and put me in the hospital for an operation. This was a year before I would be taken to school.

The condition of my legs was bad. They were getting locked, and I could not straighten them anymore. As a result of this, I could not stand but could only sit and crawl to get about. The doctors said they would fix my legs and at least make them straight so that I would be able to stand and eventually walk on crutches.

I thank God for my uncle. He was such a brave man, especially when the matter concerned me. He did not hesitate; he signed all the papers for my operation, and everything went well.

As soon as the wounds from the operation were healed, I was given one of those straps made of metal and leather to wear all the time, with special shoes that went from the feet straight up to the hips. I was able to walk on my own with crutches. At this time, I was not using a wheelchair yet, because the doctors had said that since my upper body seemed strong, I could use crutches, and I used those long ones that would come up to armpits.

When it was time to go to school in 1978, I remember how my uncle carried me on his back, with the chitenge material wrapped around me, like our mothers in Zambia would carry their babies. It was quite a distance from where we lived to the bus station, and when we reached Luanshya, we had to walk from the station to the school.

I went to the Da-Gama Special School for the Handicapped in Luanshya Town, which is southwest of Kitwe where my uncle lived, to start my grade 1. This school was a special boarding school for disabled children, and it was run by the Roman Catholic nuns.

It was from that school that I did grade 1 to grade 3. There were few disabled school children, only about 49 of us, since the school also was new, and we were the second intake. There was only one class for each grade. I should confess, though, it was my first time to see so many children who were also disabled like me.

To tell the truth, I was so surprised and at the same time comforted, in a way, to learn and realize that I was not alone. If I can also remember, there were about 29 boys and 20 girls in the entire school. We had two separate dormitories. We also had two caretakers, one for each dormitory and use to call them "mothers" because they were responsible for making sure we took a bath every day, and that we looked clean and neat all the time.

Sadly, however, this school only went up to grade 3. When we reached and completed grade 3, we were discharged from this school and encouraged to continue school elsewhere in any other ordinary school. To be honest, I was so sad when it was time to leave this school.

I got so used to being in an environment where I felt accepted, loved, and wanted. This was a wonderful place to me because everyone was almost like me, and we could relate to each other as disabled people so well. We had the feeling of going out in the world where the reality we all knew would be harsh for a disabled person. It was not a good feeling.

In my case, when this time came, I went to live with my uncle who was a teacher. He was the one who had loved me in Kitwe for a year, and that is where I did my grade 4 in Chimwemwe Township. Later in the following year, I moved to join my parents and family in Chingola.

It was only sometime later when I was in Chingola, a town northwest of Kitwe, when I started having difficulties with my crutches and those special shoes, and I started using a wheelchair.

When my crutches and shoes got worn out, my dad again would not buy me new ones, even when he was working. My mother had to take me to and from school on her back every day for three months.

I really sympathized with Mum. By this time, I was a big and heavy boy. I was now in grade 5. That is when a women's charitable club, in which the deputy headmistress of my school was a member, donated my first wheelchair ever. A wheelchair came as a major blessing, really, a great relief for my mother.

Winston spreads the Good Word at his home church in Kitwe.

Allow God to Decide

The new reality of rural life

In 1985, my father decided to take an early retirement from his work. He and Mum decided that we should all move from town and go to live with our grandparents, in a village in the rural area near my mother's family home in Kabwe.

We lived in Chingola then, one of the mining towns in Zambia in the Copperbelt Province. It was a long trip for all of us, especially for the children. There were about five of us then. I was the oldest, and the youngest of the group was about 4 years old.

On that day, we started off by bus early in the morning, from Chingola to Kitwe, which took us an hour or so. We had to wait on the railway station until evening to get onto the train. From there, we traveled from Kitwe to Kabwe, which took us the whole night to reach Kabwe the next morning. From Kabwe Town Centre, we had to get into a lorry truck to reach the farm. It also took us almost the whole day to reach our grandparent's farm. We were really exhausted when we finally reached our destination.

At the farm, we were faced with the new reality of rural life. There was no electricity, no running water, and no flush toilets, as we had become used to in town. When answering the call of nature, all you needed to do was to run to the bushes nearby and do what you had to do.

As if that was not bad enough, the place was so sandy it was hard to move about in a wheelchair. I usually failed to manage by myself but needed some back up of at least one or two people to get anywhere I wanted to go.

However, with time, we all got used to rural life at the farm. I must admit, I also learned new skills by observing some agricultural techniques, and I also discovered how people got by in a rural setting. They helped each other and learned from each other, both in modern ways and in the traditional ways of farming, using animals and machines. I observed most of them were still using primitive homemade tools like hoes and axes to prepare their fields.

In summer, people would have their small vegetable gardens near the streams, and in the rainy season, which is from November to about March, people would grow mostly maize from which we would get flour to make nshima, which is our staple food in this part of Africa.

It was during this time also that I could spend a lot of time with my grandparents, and so I became very fond of them, especially my grandmother. I was drawn to her because of her kindness, understanding and above all, her love for the Lord. We all used to call her Mama Beatrice. I learned that she was given that English name by my grandfather (from the white missionaries who first came to preach and establish the work of God at the Musofu Mission of the Seventh Day Adventist Church in the early 1900's). She was named Beatrice meaning the "blessed one" because of her devotion to things of God in Ndova, rural Zambia.

Somehow there was this bond that developed between me and my grandmother and we became close, more than I even did with my own mother. I loved her dearly and she loved me too. Of all her grandchildren, I am the only one she would call her own special child. That is how close we were, and it is because of her that I embraced Christianity easily at a young age when I was just about 13 years old.

Sadly, I lost her when I was about to go into my 7th grade at school. However, the seed of hope in the Lord Jesus Christ was already sown in me through the many times she would spend sharing the word of God with me.

I still remember how she would sit us down around the fireplace in the evening, all of us children together, and would start by telling Bible stories. Then we would all sing gospel songs so loudly and for so long on Fridays that even other children would hear us in the nearby villages and would come and join us. In fact, the night she died we sang a lot with her not knowing that was our goodbye moment. She died that same night.

It is also during this time when my grandmother was still alive when I used to have these recurring dreams of me preaching in front of congregations of white people. In the mornings, I would ask her what the meaning of these dreams would be.

"Well," she would say after a long pause, "the preaching part is okay but be careful; these white people cannot be trusted." She would always say that. I now understand her lack of trust in the white people because many had things happened to our old people back then in colonial times in Zambia.

The slavery experiences that some went through even in Zambia were part of our family history. However, little did I know that this dream would become a reality 40 years later. When I first came to the United States in 2012, I found myself preaching in an all-white church and I was the only person there who was black. Soon, I was called to travel to many other churches preaching everywhere to white people in churches throughout Melbourne, Sebastian, Vero Beach and Fort Pierce.

I must admit that not everything was bad about the coming of white people to Zambia, even in the days of my grandparents. There were always both bad and good white people who came to Zambia. One of the many good white people who came at that time, and whom we all love and cherish as Zambians, is Dr. David Livingstone, who was sent to Africa by the London Missionary Society.

He first went to South Africa but later he decided he wanted to come north into Zambia. In that time, most white people feared coming all this way into the heart of Central Africa, where Zambia is now, because of the hordes of mosquitoes that were found in these areas that caused malaria.

However, this brave white man managed to reach Zambia, and came over to visit and then to settle. It is he who with other missionaries opened the Zambia of today to Christianity, trade and commerce. He was the first European to see our magnificent waterfall and he renamed it the Victoria Falls.

In 1873, he died in our country and was found dead on his knees. Many believe he was praying for us and our country, Zambia. He died in a hut somewhere in the Chitambo Village in the Serenje district.

Before Livingstone came, the Arab traders who were mostly Muslim were already frequenting the Zambian route to trade and buy slaves, and to convert people to Islam along the way. David Livingstone's coming was a blessing because it blocked and stopped the Islamic influence from continuing.

After he died, many Christian missionaries flooded Zambia in every area of our country. To honor this man, of the five cities we have right now, Lusaka, Ndola, Kitwe, Chipata, one of them is named after David Livingstone and it is called the City of Livingstone. It is the tourist capital of Zambia in the southern province. As someone who was bred and raised in Zambia, I was at one point tempted to think that all white people were blessed and whatever they touched prospered. I was so naïve until I started to travel outside of Zambia, and especially now that one foot is in Zambia and the other in the United States.

I have come to appreciate the fact that success has nothing to do with the color of one's skin but more to do with getting the education that helps us think outside the box.

We need to start modestly with our education any way we can, and then build on that steadily. God will not let us down. I believe education is the key to progress. Embrace education, always remembering you are a child of God, and you will be amazed by what God will do through you.

A healthy field of maize (corn) on Winston's farm.

It Is Not What We Think

I guess endurance and refusing to give up in
life are lessons all of us should learn.

In 1986, I experienced what I would call a double tragedy, in a sense, because it is in that year that I lost my grandmother, the one person I loved so much and who loved me dearly. Her great worry long before she died was who was really going to take care of me when she died.

For her, even my mother, her daughter, was not able to manage me because deep down in her heart she knew that my dad did not like me. She too, like everyone else, never thought that one day I would be able to look after myself, and even have a family of my own. She did not believe that was possible, and I should confess I also felt the same.

In the same year, my parent's house burned down. The house in which we all lived caught fire, and everything burned with it. My parent's house was one of those African traditional houses made of mud-brick walls. It had a grass-thatched roof woven by our local neighbors. Everything in that house was destroyed by the fire.

On that particular day, my sister, Maria, who was about 4 years old, was with friends playing and practicing their cooking skills. The cooking was a serious one, because they had made fire using the firewood that they themselves had gathered from nearby.

The children were on the veranda of the house. Nobody was home to watch them that evening. They were alone.

Nobody knows what happened next, but we all assumed that as they were cooking, the grass-thatched roof, which was quite low, must have caught fire accidentally. All the other people were working in the fields somewhere. That is how we lost the house and everything in it. We were left with nothing but the clothes we were wearing.

I was at school and so were many school-going

children. To our shock and surprise, we saw this big, thick, dark cloud of smoke floating up in the skies from our village at a distance, as we were coming from school and about to cross the Mondake stream. By the time we were close to home, it was too late.

When I looked up and saw that smoke, my heart started beating hard. I knew for sure something was wrong. By the time we all reached home, the roof had collapsed, and there was nothing we could do to save anything from the blaze.

We stood there and watched hopelessly, crying and weeping. As for the Matafwalis, it was like a funeral because one thing was for sure. We were reduced to homelessness. We had come as a family so optimistically from town a few years ago. There and then some actions had to be taken because of what had happened. Quickly and sensibly decisions had to be made.

In the end, my family resolved that we had to relocate back to town from the farming village. This time we moved back to Kitwe. At least while we were there, my father would look for some work and start again to buy basic things that we needed as a family.

I did not know, of course, that in God's own time, I would be able to meet Mrs. Gloria Jones. Sometime later, however, behind the scenes, God was pushing us as a family to my destiny. The helpers, in this case, were members of the Jones family, who were living in Kitwe, Zambia at that time.

In my case, it was not possible for me to go with my family right away, because I was in an examination class in grade 7, and at the end of that year, I was supposed to sit for an exam. So, the family decided I would remain behind and join the family later, after I had written the national exam. I remained behind with my grandfather while the rest of my family left for Kitwe.

My time with my grandfather, my goodness, was the most difficult and challenging time of my life. To begin with, my grandfather was not a person who stayed at home all the time. He was always on the move. He was a small businessman who used to go away into the town of Kabwe, about 27 kilometers away from his farm, to sell fresh vegetables. He would be away from home five days a week.

I had to learn to fetch firewood by myself from the woods, and water from the stream, because there was no borehole in the village nearby. I also had to learn how to prepare my own meals and wash my own clothes in the stream.

When my grandfather was not home, I had to spend the nights alone in that big dark house of his because there was no electricity there yet. It was so scary at night, especially with all the noises and echoes of bats and owls coming from outside. The house was in the middle of a small forest. You could imagine what would have been racing in the mind of a young person of about 13 years of age. However, I soon got used to it.

Unfortunately, something I feared the most happened. My wheelchair broke down completely due to the rough terrain in that place. When that happened, I had no other choice but to resort to crawling as the only means to go wherever I wanted.

I had to crawl like a baby. I had to get to school every day as well using my bare hands, with nothing to protect my knees. I covered a long way to and from school every day. My hands and knees would hurt badly. I would even develop bruises on my hands and knees. But I just had to learn to live with it.

I was determined not to give up school. However, I must confess, there were times when I would break down and cry on my way to school.

But you see, God is always seeing what is happening to us, and it is in times of need and pain like this one that He will send people our way to walk and stand with us each step of the road.

At that time, God sent into my life a wonderful man who was my class teacher, Brother Emmanuel Chama, a Catholic brother from the Marist Brothers Mission from St. Paul's Catholic Mission Center.

He used to come from there to teach at our local school, Mondake Primary School. He was indeed such a pillar of strength that God gave me during the entire year of primary school. Brother Emmanuel encouraged me not to quit school but to carry on despite the many challenges I was going through.

These two people, my uncle and this teacher, really helped me to see the need for education and the opportunities education could bring into one's life (especially those of us living with disabilities). As disabled people, we should not be hidden away or locked up inside the house, but instead be encouraged and taken to school. We should not be left out at any level of development.

By October in the second week of 1986, I had finished with my grade 7 exams and was ready to join the rest of my family in Kitwe. Looking back, that whole year seemed too long for me, maybe because of the hardship I went through.

But what a relief when I went to Kitwe. In Kitwe, I found my family living in servant quarters with one bedroom but with at least a living room. My dad had found two jobs. He was working as house servant in the day and as a security guard in the night as a way of cushioning the high cost of living in town, and to top up the salary he was getting as a house servant.

Things in life may appear to be so challenging that we may want to give up our dream, even when we are almost there.

There is one African story that I will always remember, a story my grandfather once told me.

There was a bush pig that was caught in one of those rope traps that the hunters set. The bush pig tried not to cry out in the night because crying would attract people's attention, including the attention of the hunter who set the snare.

As the bush pig was struggling in the night, the rope was about to break completely. Unfortunately, at dawn the poor pig gave up and cried loudly because of pain. The hunter heard from his nearby village and came and killed the pig just when the rope was about to break. If only the pig had endured for one more hour, the rope would have broken, and the bush pig would have gone free.

Winston Matafwali works at the five-acre site
provided by a government program.

6

A Push From Somewhere Else

When my parents were struggling, not knowing where money to buy shoes would come from, God already had a plan.

It was three days before Christmas in 1986. On that day, in the morning, my mother decided to go and buy some vegetables for relish to go with our nshima for lunch that afternoon. To get to the vegetable market, she had to walk all the way past Kopa Street in the Riverside area of Kitwe, where Mrs. Gloria Jones used to live.

On that particular day Mrs. Jones was at home sorting out a few things, most likely in readiness for Christmas which was soon approaching. She was getting rid of a few things she did not want.

You must understand that, in Africa, we do not just

throw things away but first ask if someone may need what you want to throw away. It so happened that just as Mrs. Jones was going outside her gate with a box of outgrown shoes, my mother was also passing by.

Mrs. Jones asked if my mother could use the box she had, which was full of children's shoes and toys. My mother gladly accepted and off to home she went with her treasures.

When Mother got home, you should have seen just how excited we children were about the box and how eager we were to find out what was in there. Soon we discovered that there were shoes and all sorts of toys in that box. My two sisters quickly started to try on some of those shoes, and they were lucky. They did find shoes which perfectly fit them. But my younger sister, Susan, managed to find only one shoe her size. The other shoe of the pair was missing.

"If only we could find this missing shoe, then there would be no need to buy your sister school shoes," Mother said. My sister was to start school in grade 1 in that following year, 1987. She had the school uniform already bought for her, but she did not have shoes. In

Zambia, it is a requirement of every school-going child to wear a uniform with black shoes.

"I have to go and see that madam," Mother said finally. "Perhaps I could plead with her to look for that shoe in the house." However, it was easier said than done. How could my mother go alone to see Mrs. Jones when she could not speak English? How would she communicate with her?

That was the challenge. I happened to be her only child who could speak English, but I also didn't have a wheelchair at the time that I could use to go with her. However, my younger brother came up with an idea of using a wheelbarrow. He and Mother would push me.

The next day, the four of us, Mother, my brother, my sister who needed the shoe, and I, started off to see Mrs. Jones. We were warmly welcomed by Mrs. Jones, and she even gave us some food and tea served by Mrs. Jones herself, not by her servants.

However, we were all surprised that her whole attention soon shifted on me, even when I tried to explain that the purpose of our visit was to ask her to help us find the missing shoe. Of course, she went inside her house to look, but afterwards came back and said that she could not find it. She would continue looking. However, she did ask my brother and me to come back the following Sunday after church.

She did not find the missing shoe unfortunately, but she bought my sister a brand-new pair of the school shoes she needed.

God indeed works in many ways to meet our needs through people we may not even know. When my parents were struggling, not knowing where money to buy shoes would come from, God already had a plan.

While I also did not know what God was doing behind the scenes, I also thought I was helping my mother by offering to speak for her and my younger sister. God's main concern and interest was to get me connected to Mrs. Jones.

While I may have taken this relationship lightly at the time, God saw that it was to be of serious importance: to bring about his plan for my life. Who really can understand the ways of God?

I Did It

Education was my only hope.

When, finally, the grade 7 results came out in early 1987, I was on top of the moon when I learned that I was selected to go to St. Paul's School, the one school I really hoped to go to. It was one of the best missionary boarding schools in the country, run by the Marist Brothers from Spain, in the Roman Catholic Church in Zambia.

St. Paul's was a boy's secondary school then, and the best at the time in the entire central province of my country. The discipline and the pass rate at this school was second to none. No wonder most of the government officials and wealthy people loved to take their children to this school.

I was so thrilled that I had made it, but on the other hand, it was another huge challenge as far as my parents were concerned. Buying all the things I needed for school was especially difficult now that I was going into a boarding school.

Hardly a few months ago they were struggling to buy school uniforms and shoes for my sister. Now it was my turn, and they needed to find me school fees, boarding fees, buy me two pairs of new uniforms, a blanket, bed sheets, shoes, books, and groceries to last me at least a term.

It looked impossible in every way. However, yet again, as if what Mrs. Jones did for my sister by buying her those shoes was not enough, when she learned that I had passed to go to grade 8, she and fellow women friends at her church came in to help as much as they could.

She had this group from her church who were helping people in need. They used to buy big 90 kg bags of kapenta and beans, and they would repack them into smaller packs and give them out to poor people in the streets and everywhere in the compounds.

My mother was given many of those packages too. Mrs. Jones' group bought me not only blankets, bed sheets, books, and shoes, but also extra clothes and underwear to change at school. Before long, this challenge that seemed to be so huge was now manageable. I was able to report to school just in time.

At school, there were four hostels to go to, and I was sent to Clement House, the middle block. What it meant is that when you were assigned to a house hostel in grade 8, you remained in the house for the rest of your stay at that school. So, I was a Clement House student for all my school life.

Mrs. Jones also helped me get a new wheelchair to use at school instead of a wheelbarrow. Through her influence, she managed to convince her neighbor to obtain a wheelchair for me. He was a powerful man in our city of Kitwe at that time, and a medical doctor by the name of Doctor Mumba. He was president of the Rotary Club of Kitwe North.

While I was in boarding school, my life there really helped me to develop into the better person I wanted to be. I learned a lot about how to get along with people of different backgrounds, and most of all, how to manage my life without my parents watching my back all the time.

As someone who is physically challenged, I also learned how to be independent. I didn't need to depend on others for almost everything I needed. Boarding school life shaped me into the person I wanted to be, because I discovered on my own how to overcome the day-to-day challenges I faced as a person in a wheelchair.

However, in as much as I enjoyed school life, I did not know how to handle failure. School for me was okay if I did well in class. I was very much afraid of being a failure in life, because right from the beginning, when I was a small boy, my uncle who loved me so much (and even carried me to school on his back) used to tell me that education was my only hope. Therefore, each time I did not do well, I would say to myself that I was failing. That would take me into some serious thinking and eventually into depression because I would think that my disability had everything to do with failing in school.

I used to think that now polio was affecting my ability to perform. I wanted to have a family one day, and I also wanted to be able to do things with my life, and education was the solution I had been given.

Sometimes my dad would even point at the disabled people who would be begging in the streets and say to me, "Do you want to end up like them?" Please do not get me wrong. That was good advice, but he was simply adding salt on the open wounds inside me, because I was hurting from the wounds and failure.

The problem I really had was I did not have someone I could open up to, someone who would help me to see things going on in my mind in the right way. What was really happening was, when I excelled everyone would rally around me, but when I was failing, I was left along to sort myself out.

I was really hurting each time I encountered failure along the way because I did not know what to do. However, I want to thank God, because even in the midst of all this confusion happening in my mind, I did manage to finish secondary school and later college education.

In Zambia, we have years of learning all together. Seven of these years are for primary school education and five years for secondary school education, and then after, of course, one can enter college or university if you qualify according to examination results.

Winston delivering a message about his missionary work.

I Let Go of All the Pain and Frustration

It was real and tangible. It was as though someone was washing me from the inside and getting rid of things.

Without realizing it, I had often let self-pity, bitterness, lack of forgiveness, resentment and the fear of failure get the better of me. I began to feel so empty that all I sometimes wanted was to die, because I got so tired of living as a cripple.

I lost interest in life because I had no purpose for living. Sometimes, all I ever thought of was to die. I did not then understand that what I needed to learn was to trust in the Lord Jesus Christ as a child of God. He alone is the only truth in our lives, not all the worries I had.

I needed to know the truth from the truth Himself,

because He is also the way, the truth and the life. Even with regard to my own body that I hated so much and used to complain about, I needed to understand that the Lord Jesus Christ does not look at the outward appearance, but the Lord looks at the heart.

However, I would deceive myself by thinking that if only I could find someone who would accept me as a physically challenged person and love me, I would be fine. But that did not work either. I got married to a lovely lady, but after some time, I still felt so empty.

While I was born and raised on the Copperbelt province, Tizi spent most of her childhood in the Eastern Province of Zambia and Sinda District in particular. It was in Sinda rural area where a white catholic priest first saw Tizi and got so concerned that she was not in school.

The priest did not waste time but quickly arranged to meet with Tizi's parents and discussed having Tizi enrolled in school. However, this idea was met with challenges such as the distance and Tizi's physical disability. The nearest school was still far away, making it difficult for Tizi to manage going to school on her own like the other school children, who would walk to school.

On second thought, the priest suggested taking Tizi to Lusaka Cheshire Home. Thank God Tizi's parents agreed and that is how she found herself at Lusaka Cheshire Home.

Cheshire Home

There are centers in a few places in Zambia where school-going disabled children are taken for school and are equipped with various skills.

At the time these centers were run by the Catholic sisters and when the priest finally took Tizi to Lusaka, the sisters were happy to have her. She progressed well in school there, except the school had classes only from grade one to grade three. When she passed to go to grade four, she was transferred to Ndola Cheshire Home and Ibenga primary school where she advanced up to Secondary School at Ibenga Girls.

It was at Ndola Cheshire Home that I first met Tizi years later.

Something sadly struck me, in as far as disabled women getting married is concerned. While "able-bodied" men would secretly have a girl friend who was disabled, they were not willing to marry them or even take responsibility in case of pregnancy because they were too ashamed of how society will look at them.

I saw many single, disabled young mothers whose so-called able-bodied men had run away and had nothing to do with them when they were pregnant. So, from that time as a young person I made it my purpose to marry a fellow disabled person and at least make a difference, instead of running away from my own people (disabled people).

One day I happened to be visiting Ndola Cheshire home to see for myself the great work the Catholic sisters were doing among disabled young people. I took notice of this beautiful young lady, Tizi. After getting to know each other for more than a year, we decided to get married in 1995.

Yet again I would say to myself, "If only I could have a child of my own, I would feel better," but still nothing really was working for me. I needed to empty myself first of what was eating me up, the pain, bitterness, self-pity, loneliness, lack of forgiveness, resentment and all that and allow God Himself to fill the whole of that emptiness with his love.

I needed to reach out to Him just like the Bible encourages us to when it says, "Knock and the door will be opened; seek and ye will find." *(Matthew 7:7) NIV.* My heart was focusing on the things that only temporarily satisfy us.

In the year 1999, I got fed up with life completely, and I attempted committing suicide many times. All that time nothing worked out either. All the attempts failed.

This time Mrs. Jones was no longer living in Kitwe. She and the rest of the family had moved to Lusaka, the national capital of Zambia. I was in Kitwe by myself with my wife and our first-born son, Winston Jr. We were staying in a rented small house in Luangwa Shanty Compound. Our son was just about 2 years old. I realized I was hurting myself and those around me and decided to approach God differently. I was 31 years old then.

I stopped asking God to kill me, but instead let go

of all the pain and bitterness in me and surrendered my whole life entirely to the Lord Jesus Christ. I knew God as the Lord Almighty and creator, and that he could do about anything He wanted. But even that was not enough. I needed to know him more.

I therefore decided to seek the Lord in a deeper and more serious way, and I started praying all night long alone for three weeks without stopping, not even for a single night. I prayed to God to show me his purpose for my life, and I would say to God, "Speak to me."

For the first two weeks, nothing happened, but I was determined to continue praying and pushing on until something happened. I would not sleep at night, but I would wait for everyone to fall asleep and would start praying and pleading all night long for God's help.

It was in my third week when one night I suddenly felt the anointing presence of God come upon me. It was real and tangible. It was as though someone was washing me from the inside and getting rid of things. At the same time there was a sense of filling up from my head to my toes.

As this was happening, I was shedding tears of joy, and at the same time, it was like I was being freed from all the pain, bitterness and everything that had held me prisoner. For the first time in my life, I accepted my disability. The question of "Why me?" was changed to the "Why not me?"

I started laughing and my wife was awakened by my laughing in the night. She thought there was something going wrong with my mind, but I assured her I was okay.

That was my turning point and from that time I have not looked back. I no longer look at myself as someone who is not good enough but as someone who is fearfully and wonderfully mad, because that is what the Bible says about me.

From that time, I have come to know God in a much deeper way. He is not only my Creator but is my Father too and He cares and loves me so much. From that moment, I also said to God, "Send me wherever you want me to go, and I will go." He said to me in the same way that He touched me with love, He wanted me to share this hope with others. I did not wait to go to Bible school, but I openly shared the word of God and the testimony of my encounter with God that night to whoever I met in the streets and in my community.

I shared the good, the bad and the ugly things of my life, and true to God's word, it is truly in the areas where we have been weak that God will anoint us with his strength.

Wherever I went I shared the gospel, tears streaked down the cheeks of the people I spoke to, because it was no longer my voice that they heard, but His voice within my voice. My fellow disabled people recognized in me their own fears and failures and gave their lives to Lord Jesus Christ. Before long, people in the streets would call me "Pastor" and I got very busy for the Lord.

In the meantime, when we moved from the Luangwa Shanty Compound to Parkland's Kitwe, my wife and I joined this wonderful man who was just starting his church in his house, Pastor Emmanuel Shikaputo. I served in that church for fourteen years. This man loved us and helped us a lot in understanding many things of God.

We love him too. I served in that King's Garden Church faithfully as an ordinary member to start with, just like everyone else, and then as a cell-group leader, then Elder and as an Associate Pastor, up to the time we started our own ministry in 2014.

There was a period of about three years between 1997 to about 2000 while we were still in Luangwa when I lost touch with Mrs. Jones. She was also going through a transition after leaving Lechwe School where she had been working as a Deputy Head in Kitwe.

She took up a position as Director of Studies in Baobab College in Lusaka. At the same time, my elder sister was going through a divorce, so she could not help me either like Mrs. Jones would always do. It is at this time I had no one to lean on. That is the time when God got my attention and He helped me.

I learned in that period to look up to God, where all our help really comes from. It is at that time when I also joined a group called Mighty Women and Men of Valor. This group prays and fasts every Thursday from 10:00 in the morning to evening (16:00) every week in Zambia. This group really taught me to pray and fast, and how to develop a relationship with God.

However, it was not long before Mrs. Jones sent a friend from Lusaka to look for me, and we got back together again. I would visit her in Lusaka with my entire family and we would stay in her house for weeks.

9

I Can Do All Things Through God Who Strengthens Me

We have witnessed the power of God in our lives

The gospel we preach extends beyond the eternal hope we have because Jesus rose from the dead and restored mankind to God. It is the gospel that empowers us as we live here and now, and its truth will invade every area, where we allow Christ to impact us in our lives.

In Luangwa Shanty Compound, I had been renting a small one-room house with a dirt floor. It had no running water, and we would get our water from a hand-dug well outside. It also had no modern toilet but a hand-dug pit latrine also outside. The room where the pit latrine was, was the same room used as a bathroom.

You could be bathing with your bucket of water in

one corner and a strong smell from the feces down there is also coming directly on you. It was so difficult to manage for my wife and I because we are both disabled, so we started praying and believing God would somehow help us to get our own house or a better place to live in. The Lord started lifting us up bit by bit.

By 2001, we moved to Parklands, a beautiful place where wealthy people live, but lived in servant's quarters where we were renting a house. It was still a small house, but it had running water, a toilet inside and electricity. We never stopped there but continued praying for our own house.

We did not know that Mrs. Jones, who had moved to Lusaka, was also being troubled in her mind about us not having a house of our own. We learned later that one day in 2003 she was watching our National TV in Zambia, when she saw the story of a woman who was at the railway station. She used to sleep there in the cold with her small children because her husband had deserted her for another woman. She was left her with five small children to look after in a rented house.

She was evicted by the landlord after many months

of failing to pay the rent. She did not have money or anywhere to go, and so she decided to go to the railway station to the waiting room to sleep with the children in the cold season while she was thinking of what to do next.

Her parents were in Mongu Town extremely far away, where she could have gone by train. But she did not have the money for the train fare. It was at this point, while still watching this story on TV that Mrs. Jones got worried again about me and the children not having our own house.

"What if in the future we failed to pay our rent?" she thought. It was very cold in Zambia that year and Mrs. Jones really felt sorry for this poor mother. Immediately she found a way of getting in touch with me. She asked me to start looking for a house on sale which she would buy for us. We found this house in which we are now living in Kwacha East. She sent the money and we bought it.

It was a one-bedroom, small house at first, but she started extending it bit by bit starting with a bedroom for the children, a kitchen and a living room. Over a long period of time, we eventually had a comfortable home. Mrs. Jones helped us to achieve that long before she even came to the United States.

I built a front porch with concrete and broken mosaic tiles dumped as useless in a contractor's yard. So, we had a little balcony to sit on in the fresh air in the cool of the evening.

In late 2017, we bought a cheap, second-hand car to be used for my ministry, especially in the rainy season when a pastor in a wheelchair cannot move at all to visit the sick, the dying or to the pulpit-preaching commitments. God indeed has turned around our lives over the years. We have witnessed the power of God in our lives, and we can rightly say now that we can do all things through Christ who strengthens us.

Gloria Jones

10

My Bible College Times

When Mrs. Jones came over to Kitwe to say goodbye, I thought I would never see her again. But I was grateful to God for bringing her into our lives and for what she had done in our lives already.

In 2008, I enrolled in Bible College for my three-year program in theology, even without having enough money for me to finish the whole program. But my family and I looked to God. I had only enough for a semester and promised the director that I was going to be paying as school progressed.

However, in the second semester I reported to college without any money. I had not shared with anyone that I had difficulty raising the money. However, a miracle happened. At break time I was called to the director's office three days after school opened.

I was so scared because I had not paid my fees, therefore I did not know what was going to happen. However, I was surprised when the director told me she had called to inform me that she had a sponsor from the United States who was willing to sponsor me for the rest of the three-year program. I knew God was wanting me in Bible School.

In the first year of our college, we were all required as students to go out and do missions for at least two weeks. Since we were all from the Copperbelt, we were asked to go to serve in the Northern Province in a rural district, which I did. In the second year, we were required to go outside our own country and again serve for two weeks of mission work. I went to Congo, north of Zambia.

In the third year, there was a huge challenge thrown at us as students. This time we were asked to go outside of Africa, to another continent to do a pastoral internship for three months. The idea was to help students to get a feel of what it is like to do a ministry in a new place, in a new culture altogether. However, as in all the other journeys we had made before, we were to find our own air tickets and connections as to where to go. We only had to inform the school in good time so that the college would be aware of where we would be serving.

Mrs. Jones at this time had retired from teaching. She had even over-stayed because even at 70 years she was still active, and the Board of Directors at Baobab College wanted her to stay. When she finally retired at the age of 80, she went to the United States to stay near her daughter, Bethan, who was teaching in Florida.

When Mrs. Jones came over to Kitwe to say goodbye, I thought I would never see her again, but I was grateful to God for bringing her into our lives and for what she had done in our lives already. It was hard to accept that she was leaving Zambia for good.

Little did I know that, like Joseph in the Bible who was sent to Egypt in advance to help his family, Mrs. Jones was also going to the United States in advance to help me in my future. When this challenge and opportunity of going to another continent presented itself, I said to myself, "Wait a minute. I could speak to Mrs. Jones in the United States and see what could be worked out."

After I explained to her what I needed for this, she promised to talk to the local pastor in the United States and get back to me later. Within a week, she called me and told me I could come to the United States.

However, the challenge was not over yet. There was the issue of a visa that I had to obtain, and I could not get one easily. I had to go for an interview as well, and then afterwards, we had to talk about an expensive air ticket.

To get a visa in Africa, especially in a developing country like Zambia, to go to the United States is not easy because the Consul at the embassy would always think you will never come back (because of the many opportunities that are in the United States).

So, they make sure that they make the right decision before they grant you the visa. If necessary, some background investigations are made. Therefore, when I went to Lusaka to be interviewed at the American Embassy, I was sent back home. I was told they were going to call me back when they were ready for me for another interview. They kept me in the dark because they did not tell me when they would call me.

To get a visa that time I had to take two trips to Lusaka. Thank you, God. In the end, I did get a visa, and now there was the challenge of raising the money for the air ticket. I needed about $2,300 for the return ticket.

All this time, my family and I were praying, and I was fasting because that was a huge test of our faith. We have never had that amount of money ourselves. Therefore, we had to borrow a lot of money and even had to surrender the title deeds of our house for us to get all the money.

I promised our lenders, I was going to pay them back when I returned from the United States after three months, and they eventually lent us the money.

I was the first student in our college, in the ten years since our college was started, to try to do what I managed to do in 2012, going all the way from Africa to do my internship in another continent. Truly, even in my condition in a wheelchair, we can do all things through Christ who strengthens us.

I came back from the United States with more than enough money and I paid off all my debts, because Mrs.

Jones raised money by producing concerts, where her music students performed. The people at the United Church of Sebastian supported me faithfully when fundraising events for my mission took place. It is thanks to them that I am a fully qualified pastor today.

11

I Will Insist I Am the One for Whom God Had a Plan

Take your eyes off your problem and focus on the good and the loving Father who has great plans for you.

In the Bible there is a very interesting story. I can relate to it as someone who has been living with a physical disability myself, and I remember well the early challenges my parents and I went through.

However, in that story there is a man who was blind from birth. He was brought to the Lord Jesus. The people wanted to find out from Jesus who had really sinned to cause that man to be blind. The question was, "Was it his parents, or he himself?" (*John 9:1, NIV*).

Jesus' answer was that it had happened that way so that the works of God might become known, or in another way of putting it, so that the glory of God could be seen.

"What glory of God could be seen in a disability?" we may ask ourselves. When you may also have a situation that you don't understand and wonder, "Why is it like that?" Be strong. God knows better than you about you and your situation. He will not let you down.

Who thought I would ever become a pastor and be a blessing to my family one day? Take your eyes off your problem and focus on the good and the loving Father who has great plans for you.

Getting back to our story, it was not long before everyone saw what Jesus did in this man's life.

You are a miracle in the making and in God's own time, He will display his grace in you for all to see in the presence of God. People change. As you linger in God's presence, something is happening to you, and you will not be the same person. Therefore, hold on to the Lord as the child of God you really are. Keep busy for the Lord and do not say there is nothing you can do for God. Start small and do not be afraid to begin just where you are. Accept who you are because God works with inadequate people, and He works through them to do wonderful things. God will never leave you or forsake you.

I feel strongly that I have been called to minister to the poor, the rejected, the outcasts and those forgotten by society because in addition to myself relating to those groups of people, I have always, in my ministry as a pastor, been drawn to them.

God himself has brought them into my life many times, and many of the people that I have in my church today are people that have come to find me, as opposed to me seeking them out.

12

A Few Stories to Share With You

A Boy with Cerebral Palsy

I have in my church a young boy of about 12 years old. He cannot talk nor walk properly, and his fingers are cinched tight in a fist-like form in both hands. He cannot feed himself but must be fed. He and his family used to go to another big church, but other children there, and even grown people, used to laugh at him.

Therefore, his mother came and asked if the boy could come to our church because we are different and full of loving people. We immediately accepted him. The boy has ever since been regularly coming to church. The boy loves our church, and we also love him dearly.

A Woman Dying of Cancer

A young woman of about 30 years was abandoned and forgotten in a hospital and now was dying. Her brother, knowing I was a pastor, asked me to visit her at the hospital because she had been ill for a long time. She had been in the hospital for about six months because she had cervical cancer, and the disease had overwhelmed all her internal organs.

People had stopped visiting her because when you have been sick for a long time, people sometimes actually lose hope and stop visiting you. Also because of her illness, her body odor had become very unpleasant. In fact, even her brother was saying he did not know when he had last visited her.

Anyway, he gave me the hospital bed number and the room number, because she had been isolated for months.

Because she smelled very bad due to her condition, nobody wanted to enter her room. Even the nurses told me that I should not go into her room. But I did go in there, and we spent a long time together. I felt as if I had known her for a long time. I could see in her eyes she was lonely, and I was honored to spend time with her.

She passed away a day after I visited her. We had prayed together for a long time. I felt bad when I learned of her death, but at the same time, I was full of joy that I led her to the Lord just in time.

A Lady with A Skin Challenge

An albino young mother of five children one day came to my home. She was pregnant and suffering because of what she was going through as a wife and as an albino person. She had experienced a lot of pain and rejection for her entire life. Albino people in Africa get burned by the sun because most of them cannot apply expensive sunscreen to protect their skin.

It is hot, especially in the summer. Sunscreens are too expensive for an average albino person to afford. When they are burned, they develop sores that can be very painful and extensive all over their body, face, lips, and limbs.

These sores produce puss that can smell very bad.

With these sores, the person can be very unpleasant to look at, and to be with. What is even worse about what the albino is going through is that there is a superstition promoted by those who believe in and practice witchcraft in Africa.

These people believe if a body part of an albino person is taken from them, mixed with some herbal medicine and given to someone to eat who wants to get rich, they would become rich instantly.

Because of these superstitions, we have had albino people endure and arm or leg being chopped off and may albinos have been murdered. Therefore, every albino lives in fear, not knowing what is going to happen to them any day.

This woman was lonely and did not have friends or people she could trust. However, I loved her the very first time she visited our home, and I prayed for her like I was praying for my own daughter. She has joined our church and we love her very much. She is also a blessing in our ministry and church because she is highly intelligent and helps with the administration.

Needless to say, I am comfortable and honored to

serve the poor as their pastor. I have known from the start that God wants me to be the pastor for the poor. The thing is, who is really there to reach out to the rejected, the outcast, and the forgotten?

If the ministers of God only want to serve the elite and wealthy people because of what they can give back in the offering box, we must remember what our Lord, Jesus Christ, said. He also came to bring the good news to the poor. Are we, his servants, not asked to do the same?

13

How Our Church Started

The Gateway of Hope

We started and planted a church right in our living room inside our house, just my wife, our two children and myself. We had our first meetings in there for months, but as the Lord kept adding to our numbers, we moved outside into our backyard in 2014.

The name of our church is "The Gateway of Hope." It is our vision and mission that everyone, regardless of their background and status, should be given an opportunity to know Christ and enter through that gate opened by our Lord Jesus Christ Himself. At our church, offerings are not our priority, people are. We want our people to learn to love God as much as we love God's people.

Our people sometimes do not have anything to give in the offering plate, but we encourage them to give an offering of love by taking a card on which is written "I will visit someone I do not know in the hospital this week" or "I will help someone this week to clean their house or mend a fence."

We are teaching our people to learn to "Give the day to the Lord" by encouraging them to come and attend morning prayers from about 05:00 hours to 06:00 hours every workday, where we literally ask God to use us for His glory that day. We call this "The Morning Glory Time," because what we will be doing basically in the morning is tapping into God's glory for the day.

Disability or anything else should not prevent us from serving the Lord. My family and I are "wheeling" for Jesus in Africa in a wheelchair, and when all is said and done, we will insist we are the ones specially chosen to serve Him.

May this be your story too.

Becoming Somebody Who Mattered To God

Therefore, learn to get your share of God's grace by asking for it in faith. He will answer.

If you only believe that God exists, you are missing out on knowing Him. He is a rewarder of all those who earnestly seek Him. God is more than just a creator and more than just a father figure. He rewards and promotes too.

As a child of God, you and I need to know that when we are in Christ, the old has passed and gone and a new way of living has been prepared for you. You must use your gift of faith to step into this new life. Let go of your past because the past is not your future.

God knew that man's standards would focus on

the outward appearance. Whether we like it or not, we are influenced by external appearances. But we must understand that God's focus is not on the outside but on the heart of a person.

No wonder God said of David in the Bible that David was a man after God's own heart *(Samuel 16:7 NIV)*. When we really entrust all our lives to our Lord, Jesus Christ, we will be amazed by the many things he will do for us and to us.

There is nothing that God cannot do. Out of nothing He created the whole world, not only what we can see but also that which we cannot see. If we only let Him in and allow Him to be the Lord of our lives, amazing things will happen.

We should not say or think that if we are weak, God cannot use us. Remember what happened when Paul pleaded with God to remove his "thorn"? God refused and said, "My grace is sufficient for you for my power is made perfect in your weakness" *(2 Corinthians 12:9-10)*. Learn in your weakness to look to God always, just like the Israelites did every day in the wilderness. They had to actively receive and depend on God for their daily sustenance.

Therefore, learn to get your share of God's grace by asking for it in faith. He will answer. I have learned to do so as a pastor in a wheelchair because sometimes I feel weak and inadequate. When I feel like that, I ask God to be my provider and fill in my empty spaces.

God has the most amazing ways to work in the unseen details of life, and He will work out His plan for you no matter what you have been through. Say "yes" to God now. Say "yes" to whatever He brings your way. Seek Him wholeheartedly.

Surrender to what He is requiring from you and know that He is working out His wonderful plans for you right now. Behind the scenes God will always bless His people.

I am a testimony of what God can do. God has blessed us as a family so much that everyone is surprised at what God can do. Our lives have been transformed totally and it is no longer a matter of how unfortunate we have been, but how beautiful our lives have become as a family through the Lord Jesus Christ.

Indeed, the Lord God Almighty made it possible for us to stand out as proof of the power of His grace.

Conclusion

Forty years ago, who would have thought this small boy, who was being carried in a wheelbarrow because he did not have a wheelchair, would one day become a pastor, and even come to the United States to preach the blessing of God's loving kindness.

I was a person everyone thought had no hope for a future. We can only say that God indeed works in ways we cannot understand.

Gloria Jones originally traveled to Zambia with her husband, Graham, who was experienced in the electrical-supply system in the UK. He came to the African country to help develop the Zambian network.

Pastor Winston has been an important part of my life since he was a young child. I am forever grateful for all I have learned from him.

He has taught us that no disability, no difficulty, no problem should be allowed to define who you are or what you can achieve in life. He believes and lives by the philosophy that what many people would consider complete impossibilities can be "downgraded" to challenges if approached with the faith and determination to succeed.

Winston's faith is unshakeable. He knows he is a child of God, and that God has always had plans for him – that God will help him bring those plans to fruition. He believes with all his heart and soul that God intends him to be a pastor for the poor. He is not at all afraid of the prospect of living in poverty himself, and will tell you, smiling, that he is quite used to it.

The members of his church are for the most part the rejected, the disabled, the unfortunate, and those who have been abandoned by society. But, in his church they are welcome, respected and loved.

Winston finds jobs for them, so they feel needed and valuable. He has deacons, ushers, a choir. His administrator is a woman who was once shunned by everyone in the village because she is an albino, and therefore an object of superstition and fear. Now, her natural intelligence is being put to good use.

Our church in Florida tries to support him financially, but he considers himself a "channel" through which water flows from one place to another. The money he receives must flow from him in the same way, to others in his care. Their need is great.

I have known him to sit for many hours by the bedside of a dying woman, holding her hand, and easing her passing with prayers and softly sung hymns.

I have known him to laugh uproariously at the nervousness of a lifeguard at a swimming pool, who watched incredulously as he climbed out of his wheelchair and plopped awkwardly into the deep end of the pool and was immediately quite in his element (as I had taught him in my house pool in Kitwe).

I am humbled by all he is, and all he does, and am deeply grateful for the privilege of knowing him.

Gloria Jones

Mrs. Jones retired to Sebastian, Florida to live near her daughter and family, after living in Zambia for many years.

As she shared her life stories with our congregation, we all fell in love with this little boy in the wheelbarrow.

Mrs. Jones had continued to support Winston as he grew, helping him attend school and in any other way she could. Winston was now a grown man who had advanced successfully through the Zambian educational system and would soon become a pastor.

He now had a family of his own.

Our congregation felt called by the Lord to support Winston and his family, so began a long distant relationship between people in Sebastian and in Kitwe, Zambia.

Pictures, letters, emails, and phone calls began flying across the Atlantic. Winston was required to finish his pastoral degree by serving in a congregation that was not his own. Our Sebastian congregation excitedly proposed that Winston come to America to finish his studies.

After much preparation and all the necessary paperwork, all was in order, and we anxiously awaited Winston's arrival.

Winston had never traveled internationally and was truly not aware of how things worked. When we think back over his first trip, we all realize God was leading, watching over him carefully. Imagine venturing out, not knowing what to expect, sitting in a wheelchair, leaving your family and everything familiar behind.

Winston was not aware the airlines served meals and that there was no cost. He did not want to spend any money, so he politely refused any food each time the flight attendants came by. Winston did not eat at all for 26 hours. Needless to say, he was very hungry when he arrived in Florida and Mrs. Jones fed him very well!

One of the fondest memories of Winston's visit to Florida is when he came to our home for our annual Super Bowl party. Winston's eyes grew wide as he saw the spread of food all over our kitchen.

Remembering that he and his family typically ate very sparingly and never ate three meals a day like we are used to doing in the US, we felt a little embarrassed at the over-abundance of goodies. He looked it all over and was further amazed that everything sat out for everyone to enjoy during the game.

"You mean, all this food just sits here, and people come and eat whenever they want?"

"Yes, that's how it works, just like grazing cattle," replied my husband. He laughed out loud at that, shook his head and said, "You Americans!"

Then he began loading his plate with various snacks, thoroughly enjoying the food and the football. Winston was in his second home.

Julie (Hale) Maschhoff

Printed in the United States
by Baker & Taylor Publisher Services